GREEK BEASTS AND HEROES

The Beasts in the Jar

D1410463

You can read the stories in the
Greek Beasts and Heroes series in any order.

If you'd like to read more about some of
the characters in this book, turn to pages
76 and 77 to find out which other books to try.

Atticus's journey begins in this book,
and continues in *The Magic Head*.

Turn to page 79 for a complete
list of titles in the series.

GREEK BEASTS AND HEROES

The Beasts in the Jar

LUCY COATS
Illustrated by Anthony Lewis

Orion
Children's Books

Text and illustrations first appeared in
Atticus the Storyteller's 100 Greek Myths
First published in Great Britain in 2002
by Orion Children's Books
This edition published in Great Britain in 2010
by Orion Children's Books
a division of the Orion Publishing Group Ltd
Orion House
5 Upper St Martin's Lane
London WC2H 9EA
An Hachette UK company

3 5 7 9 8 6 4 2

A catalogue record for this book is available from the British Library

ISBN 978 1 4440 0065 8

Printed in China

www.orionbooks.co.uk

www.lucycoats.com

For Mary Hoffman,
with love and eternal thanks
for Being There When Needed.
L. C.

For the children and staff
of Manley Village School
A. L.

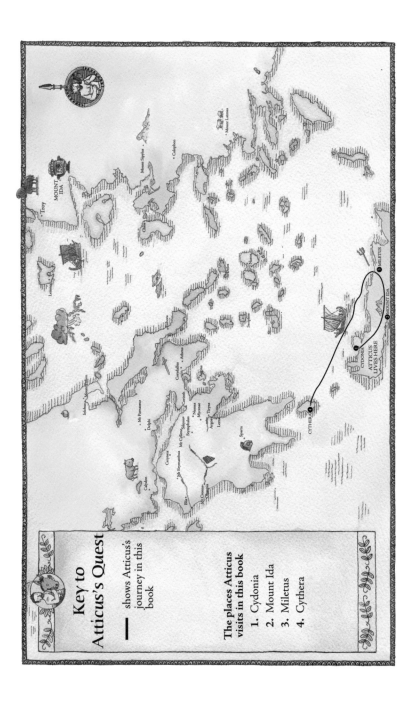

Key to
Atticus's Quest

— shows Atticus's
journey in this
book

**The places Atticus
visits in this book**

1. Cydonia
2. Mount Ida
3. Miletus
4. Cythera

Contents

Stories from the Heavens

Long ago, in ancient Greece, gods and goddesses, heroes and heroines lived together with fearful monsters and every kind of fabulous beast that ever flew, or walked or swam. But little by little, as people began to build more villages and towns and cities, the gods and monsters disappeared into the secret places of the world and the heavens, so that they could have some peace.

Before they
disappeared,
the gods and
goddesses gave
the gift of storytelling to men and
women, so that nobody would ever forget
them. They ordered that there should be
a great storytelling festival once every
seven years on the slopes of Mount Ida,
near Troy, and that tellers of tales should
come from all over Greece and from

 lands near and far to take
part. Every seven years a
beautiful painted vase,
filled to the brim with
gold, magically appeared as a first prize,
and the winner was honoured for the rest
of his life by all the people of Greece.

Atticus the Storyteller Sets Out

Now a little after those long ago times there was a sandalmaker called Atticus who lived in a little village to the east of the great city of Cydonia in Crete, with his wife Trivia, his nine children (eight girls and a boy), Melissa his donkey, Circe his pig, Scylla his cow, Phaëthon his cockerel, and twenty-four speckled hens (who had no names because the fox was always eating them).

Atticus was a very good sandalmaker, but he was an even better storyteller.

The children of the village were always popping into the shop to ask for

a quick story, and Atticus was always happy to oblige, because he claimed that the stories got into his sandals and made the feet in them walk along faster.

What Atticus really wanted was to tell his stories in the competition at the great storytelling festival of the gods at Troy.

He had never quite managed it, because on the way there he wanted to

visit the places where the gods were born, and see where all the monsters lived.

Then he wanted to sail to Troy just like the kings and princes had done in the great war.

The journey would take months, so what with the children's coughs and Scylla having a calf and Trivia having a new baby he'd never been able to spare the time before. It was now or never.

So Atticus decided that he would leave
his only son, Geryon, in charge of the
sandal shop, the girls in charge of the
animals, and Trivia in charge of everyone.

One fine morning in late autumn
Atticus packed his bags and loaded
Melissa the donkey.

He wiped his eyes and blew his nose
noisily before he hugged his wife and
children seven times for luck and set
off, shouting goodbyes and last-minute
instructions as he went.

Nine grubby handkerchiefs and one

clean one waved and waved in the distance as Atticus the Storyteller and Melissa the donkey walked down the track away from the bay of Cydonia and towards the port of Miletus.

"I hope Geryon keeps my tools sharp," he muttered. "And I wonder whether the girls will remember to shut the hens up at night. Perhaps I should just ... Melissa snorted and marched on firmly, her small hooves throwing up puffs of white dust.

"Oh well, I suppose you're right,"
sighed Atticus. "We must start, or we shall
never get there. Shall we have a story to
set us on our way?"

He looked at Mount Ida far to the
south. "Let's begin at the very beginning."

Father Sky and Mother Earth

In the time before time began there was only Gaia, the beautiful Earth, and her husband Uranus, the Sky. Uranus loved Gaia so much that he wrapped his great black cloak of twinkling stars about her, and danced her all around the heavens.

Soon they had twelve beautiful children called the Titans, who became the first gods and goddesses. But then lovely Gaia gave birth to more children, and they were not beautiful at all.

Uranus hated the ugly one-eyed Cyclopes babies as soon as he saw them, and when he was shown the hideous hundred-armed monsters that came next, he roared with rage, and locked them all up in the dreadful land of Tartarus, which lay deep in the depths of the Underworld.

Gaia was very angry, because she loved all her children whatever they looked like, and she vowed to punish Uranus.

She gave a magic stone sickle to Cronus, her youngest son, and sent him to fight his powerful father.

Cronus was dreadfully frightened, but he loved his mother, and always obeyed her.

So he hid in a fold of his father's cloak, and waited till Uranus was not looking.

Then Cronus gave Uranus such a great wound with the sickle that Uranus fled into the furthest part of the heavens and never returned.

Then Gaia married Pontus the Sea, who covered her body with his beautiful rainbow waters, and as a sign of her love for him, she gave birth to the trees and flowers and beasts and birds, and every kind of creature, including people.

And for many, many moons there was peace and harmony in every part of the earth.

By evening, Atticus and Melissa had begun
to climb the steep slopes of Mount Ida. The
village was an invisible dot on the horizon
behind them. There was a huge cave above
them, with a great stone lying beside it.

"That reminds me of another story
about Cronus. Would you like to hear it?"

Melissa gave a hee-haw, and tossed
her head.

The Stone Baby

Cronus now ruled over all that was, and soon he married his sister Rhea, the most beautiful of all the Titans. But he always remembered what he had done to his father Uranus, and he was frightened that one of his own children might do the same to him.

So as each child was born, he opened his enormous mouth wide, wide, wide and swallowed it in one big gulp.

Rhea was very sad that she could never see her children, and she tried to persuade Cronus to let her keep just one. But Cronus just shook his head and patted his big belly.

"They are quite safe in here, my dear," he boomed. "I can feel them all wriggling around!"

Rhea decided to ask Gaia for advice.

"When the next child is born, you must play a trick on Cronus," said Gaia. "You must get an enormous stone, and wrap it up just like a baby. Keep it beside you, and when Cronus asks you for the child, give him the stone instead, and hide the real baby somewhere safe."

So that is just what Rhea did.

She took the child (whom she named Zeus) to a cave on Mount Ida. Then she summoned some noisy sprites, and told them to play loud music around the cave mouth, so that Cronus wouldn't hear Zeus when he cried.

Cronus never noticed a thing. The baby gods and goddesses inside him grew and grew, and kicked and kicked to get out.

 24

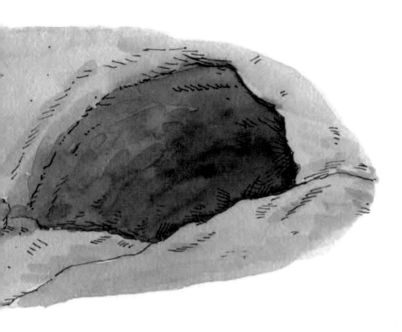

They used the heavy stone which Rhea had made him swallow as a football inside his tummy, and this made Cronus very cross and uncomfortable as he strode about his business across the heavens and around the earth.

And the rumbles his stomach made because of it were the first thunder ever heard.

The cool blue light of dawn shone on the eastern slopes of Mount Ida as Atticus and Melissa looked back. Although they had only been walking for a day the sandal shop and the family seemed far away already, and they still had a long way to go before they even reached the harbour at Miletus.

"Let's have another story to keep us cheerful," said Atticus.

King of the Gods, Lord of the Universe

Rhea sent a magical goat called Amaltheia and some of her favourite nymphs to look after baby Zeus in the cave on Mount Ida. Amaltheia's milk, which tasted of ambrosia and nectar, made him strong and tall in no time at all, and soon he was as powerful as his great father, Cronus.

When Amaltheia died, he gave her horns to the nymphs, to thank them for looking after him so well. They were magic horns of plenty, and whatever food or drink you wished for would pour out of them as soon as you asked for it. Zeus made Amaltheia's skin into magic armour, which nothing could pierce, and strode out into the world.

Rhea sent him a wife, called Metis, who was very wise. Metis told Zeus that he mustn't attack his father until he had some powerful friends to help him, and she knew just how to get them for him by a clever trick.

Zeus hid behind a tree, while Metis dressed up as an old herbwoman, and waited by the side of the road till Cronus went past.

"Try my herbs of power," she croaked. "Never be defeated! Overcome all your enemies!"

Cronus was very interested, for lately he had suspected that Rhea was plotting against him.

"I'll take some," he said, and soon
he had swallowed down a big bottle of
disgusting green liquid. It was extremely
bitter and tasted horrid.

All of a sudden he began to feel sick.
Then he was very sick indeed.

Zeus and Metis watched as first a
great stone, and then all five of Cronus's
other children, came up one by one out of
his wide, wide, wide mouth.

 29

Zeus ran out from behind his tree to join Hades and Poseidon, Hestia, Demeter and Hera, who were all furious with Cronus for trapping them for so long. Cronus took one look at their angry faces and ran away, leaving his powers behind him on the road. Zeus picked them up and put them in his pocket.

"Now I'm Lord of the Universe," he boomed.

And all the world heard him, and shivered at his powerful voice.

 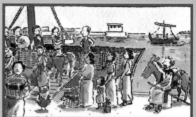

Several long days later Atticus and
Melissa reached the harbour at Miletus. It
was bustling with people as they pushed
their way through the market of fish-
sellers and clothmakers and potters. The
boat which would take them to Cythera
was bobbing up and down at the quayside
as passengers and bags and hens and ducks
and donkeys got off. There was a queue
waiting to get on.

Atticus sat on a bollard and stroked
Melissa's ears. "I'll tell you a story while
we're waiting," he said.

The Three Gifts

Now that Zeus had picked up his father Cronus's powers, he was the king of heaven and earth and everywhere in between. But even Zeus was not strong enough to look after the universe all by himself. He called his brothers to a meeting.

"I can't rule the universe properly unless you help me," he said, taking off his helmet. "Why don't we share it out between us?"

Hades and Poseidon agreed, and so into the helmet Zeus put a sapphire for the earth and sky, a turquoise for the sea, and a ruby for the Underworld.

Since Zeus was the most powerful, he closed his eyes and picked first. Out came the sapphire. Poseidon picked the turquoise and Hades the ruby. That was how the

 33

division of the universe was decided.

But the Titans, who were Zeus's uncles and aunts, did not like this at all. They thought that they should have a share in ruling things, so they raised an army to fight Zeus and his brothers.

Zeus immediately freed the Cyclopes and the hundred-armed monsters that his grandfather had imprisoned in Tartarus, to help him. The Cyclopes were so grateful that they made presents for the brothers.

For Poseidon they made a trident which could cause earthquakes and tidal waves.

For Hades they made a helmet of darkness, so that he could sneak up on his enemies without being seen.

And for Zeus they made thunder and lightning bolts which made him

 34

so powerful that no
one could stand
against him.

The Titans were soon beaten, and Zeus
banished nearly all of them to Tartarus,
where he set the hundred-armed monsters
to guard them. Prometheus and
Epimetheus, the only two Titans who
had supported Zeus, were allowed to

go free. But Atlas, the strongest of the Titans, was sent to the far ends of the earth, so that he could carry the weight of the heavens on his shoulders for ever.

At last they were on board *The Maid of Cythera*. Melissa brayed goodbye to Crete as Atticus arranged the bags along the deck of the boat.

A little girl nudged her mother. "Look, Mum! There's Atticus the Storyteller who lives next door to Auntie Hecuba!" she whispered.

Atticus smiled at her. "Would you like to hear a story, little one?" he asked.

"Yes, please! A nice scary one!"

Atticus settled down, and pointed into the far west, where the sun was setting.

"The scariest monster I know lives over there, under a great big fiery mountain. His name is Typhon, and this is his story."

The Volcano Monster

When Gaia learnt that Zeus had trapped her Titan children in Tartarus, she shook with rage. And out of her raging body there appeared two great and horrible monsters called Typhon and Echidna.

Echidna had a woman's head and arms, but her body was like an enormous fat snake, covered in warty spots and spines.

Typhon had a hundred heads, each one dripping with venom and slime. When he roared like a hundred lions or trumpeted like a herd of elephants, great rivers of boiling mud and fiery stones poured out of his mouths.

 39

When the gods saw him, they were so
frightened that they turned themselves
into animals and ran far away to hide in
the woods.

Typhon tore up enormous
mountains by the roots and he hurled

 40

them at Zeus and his brothers and
sisters, hissing like a thousand snakes.

But Zeus was brave, and he called
to the other gods to come and help him
defeat the monster.

Soon, a fierce battle raged over the earth, and everything was destroyed. The gods were tired out and nearly beaten. But as Typhon lifted Mount Etna to throw at Zeus's head, Zeus let fly one of his thunderbolts, and knocked the mountain down on Typhon's heads, trapping him for ever.

Echidna fled to a cave in southern Greece when she saw how Zeus had

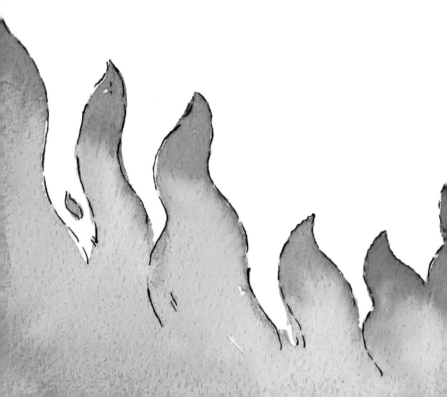

destroyed her mate. There she had her many children, all as hideous as herself, and Zeus allowed them to live in peace, so that the future heroes of Greece could fight them when the time was right.

As for Typhon, he lies wriggling and struggling under Mount Etna to this day, spewing smoke and flames out of the top, and raining down boiling stones on the poor people of Sicily.

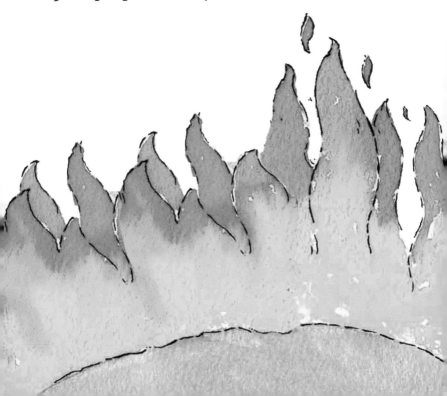

The little girl blinked sleepily up at Atticus. "Thank you. Can I have another story now?"

The other passengers looked at him hopefully. "It makes the journey go quicker," said an old lady clutching a basket of hens on her lap.

Atticus looked back towards Crete, a distant black shape in the moonlight. He thought of his family, and of his son Geryon, and how he missed them all already. There was a tower silhouetted against the horizon – a tall tower with a pointed roof.

"I shall tell you a tale of Crete," he said. "A tale of a father and son, and of how one of them reached the stars."

The Boy Who Fell Out of the Sky

King Minos of Crete was furious. He was seething. He was bubbling with rage. "Bring me Daedalus!" he cried.

Daedalus was the king's inventor, and he had designed an impossible maze to keep the king's Minotaur – a horrible bull monster – safe. Now the monster was dead, the king's only daughter had fled, and Minos wanted someone to blame.

So Daedalus was dragged before King Minos' feet in chains, and after the king had kicked him and jumped on him, he was taken to the highest room

in the highest tower in the palace at Knossos, and locked in with his son, Icarus, who was ten. They had no food, and no water, and soon they were desperately hungry and thirsty. But Daedalus was very clever, and soon he had a plan of escape.

He made Icarus climb up into the roof, where there was a big old deserted bees' nest. Icarus took all the honeycombs and threw them down to his father. Then he stole the tailfeathers from all the pigeons who were sleeping in the rafters, and threw them down too.

When they had licked some dew off the windowsills and sucked out some honey from the combs, Daedalus melted the beeswax by shining a ray of sun through a magnifying-glass he had in his pocket, and made four big wing shapes out of it.

Then, while it was still soft, he pressed the pigeons' feathers into it. He made leather straps from his belt and sandals, and then they were ready.

Daedalus and Icarus strapped their wings onto their shoulders, climbed onto the windowsill, and leaped out into the air. It was quite dark, apart from a few blazing stars, so no one could see them from the ground.

"Wheeee!" shouted Icarus, as he swept through the sky.

"I can fly! Look, Dad! I can fly!"

"Keep going west," yelled Daedalus, flapping alongside. "And remember not to fly too high. If the sun catches you when he gets up, he will melt your wings, and you'll fall!"

Icarus was having such a good time he didn't listen. He swooped up to the stars, and pulled Sirius's tail. Then he swooshed round the Great Bear. He didn't notice Helios the sun god driving his great chariot up over the eastern horizon behind him. Helios cracked his whip, and fiery rays of sunshine darted across the sky.

One of them touched Icarus's wings, and the beeswax ran like rain down into the ocean far below. A feather brushed Icarus's cheek as he tumbled helplessly to the sea beneath, crying out for his father to save him.

Poor Daedalus could only watch and weep for his lost son as he flew on towards Sicily. As his tears fell into the ocean, they were caught by the nereids and made into pearls of wisdom.

And the grandmothers, who know, say that Icarus's spirit rises up from the sea every night, and flies up to the heavens to play with the stars.

Dawn was rising over the island of Cythera as they sailed towards it, and all over the boat people were stretching and yawning as they woke up.

Atticus felt a tug on his sleeve. "Oh, all right, one last story!" he said, smiling at the little girl. "I'll tell you how fire came down to earth, and then I must see to my donkey before we get off."

How Fire Came to Earth

Zeus wanted to reward Prometheus and Epimetheus, the two Titans who had helped him in battle. So he gave them the job of making new creatures to scamper over the earth, and fill her woods and meadows with songs and joyful sounds once more.

"Here are the things you will need," he said, pointing to a row of barrels. "There's plenty for both of you."

And he flew off back to Olympus.

Prometheus set about making some figures out of the first barrel, which was full of clay. He shaped two kinds of bodies, and rolled out long sausages of mud and

pressed them against the bodies to make arms and legs. Then he made two round balls, and stuck them on the tops.

He hummed as he worked, and his clever fingers shaped ears and eyes and hair and mouths until the figures looked just like tiny copies of Zeus and his wife. It took him a very long time, because he wanted his creations to be perfect.

 54

In the time that Prometheus had made his two sorts of figures, Epimetheus had made many.

First he used up the barrels of spots, then he used all the stripes; he simply flung handfuls of bright feathers about, and as for the whiskers and claws he gave them out twenty at a time!

By the time Prometheus had finished his men and women there was not a thing left to give them other than some thin skin, and a little fine hair.

Prometheus went straight to Zeus. "My creatures are cold!" he said. "You must give me some of your special fire to warm them up, or they will die!"

But Zeus refused. "Fire is only for gods. They will just have to manage," he said. "You shouldn't have been so slow in making them."

Now this annoyed Prometheus a lot. He had taken such care, and his creations had things inside that Epimetheus could never even have thought of. So he decided to steal Zeus's fire for them.

He sneaked up to Olympus, carrying a hollow reed, and stole a glowing coal from Zeus's hearth. Then he flew down to Earth.

"Keep this sacred fire of the gods burning always," he commanded his creatures. And they did.

They looked deep into the flames and saw just what they should do. They built temples, and in each temple was a fire. And on the fires they placed offerings to the gods, and the smoke of them reached right up to Zeus's palace on Olympus.

Zeus liked the delicious smell. But when he looked down to earth and saw

the fires burning everywhere like little red stars, he was not happy at all.

"Prometheus!" he bellowed. "I told you not to take that fire! I'll make you regret your stealing ways!"

 57

He swooped down on the back of a giant eagle and carried Prometheus away to the Caucasus Mountains, where he chained him to the highest peak. And Zeus sent the giant eagle to visit him every morning and tear enormous chunks out of his liver. Every night the liver magically regrew, so that poor Prometheus's punishment was never-ending.

But Zeus never took back the gift of fire from the earth, and we have it still to warm us on cold winter nights.

Atticus and Melissa left the boat behind
and trudged along the broad track that
led across Cythera. Other donkeys passed
them on their way to the busy harbour
behind them.

"Did you ever hear the story of
Pandora's jar?" asked Atticus, looking
at the heavy jars and sacks of grain which
the donkeys were carrying.

Melissa pricked up her ears.

"No? Then I'll tell it to you."

The Beasts in the Jar

Pandora was the most inquisitive woman on earth. Zeus had made her that way on purpose. She was always asking questions and prying into other people's business.

Who's this?

What's that?

Why?

Why? Why?

she would ask her poor husband Epimetheus at least a hundred times a day.

Epimetheus was very patient, and because Pandora was so pretty and he loved her, he put up with her questions.

But one day, as she was poking about, Pandora found a great big jar right in the furthest corner of the attic. It was very heavy, and when she tried to lift it, she couldn't.

She ran down to Epimetheus, who was talking to some of the animals he had made.

"Husband! Husband!" she squealed as she saw him. "I've found a lovely big jar, and I want to know what's in it! Come and help me!"

Epimetheus went white as a sheet and began to shake.

"Wife! Wife! You must never, never touch that jar! My brother Prometheus gave it to me, and he made me promise that it must never be moved or opened

 61

till the end of the world! Promise me that whatever else you do, you will never touch that jar again!"

So Pandora promised, and although it was very difficult for her, she kept her promise for at least an hour. But then, oh dear, her curiosity began to get the better of her.

"Surely if I just have a little tiny peek, it won't do any harm!" she said.

And she sneaked up to the attic again.

Pandora quickly took the lid off the jar, and poked her nose right in. What a horrible surprise she got when a whole lot of nasty looking beasts flew out and started pricking her with their stings.

She slammed the lid back on at once, shutting inside the only creature that was left. "Oh! Oh! Oh!" she shrieked as she ran down the stairs past Epimetheus and out into the garden. "Come and get back in the jar, you horrid little things!"

But the beasts just buzzed and hummed with shrill little voices and flew off.

Ever since the day Pandora opened that jar, envy and greed and jealousy and anger and all the other evil things that were shut in there by clever Prometheus have flown about the world, stinging human beings and pricking them all over with their sharp little pins.

Only hope was left in the jar – trapped by Pandora right at the very bottom. And as long as hope is there, nothing in the world can ever be quite as bad as it seems.

 As darkness fell, Atticus knocked on a cottage door by the roadside. "I wondered if we could stop here for the night?" he asked as the door opened, and several children poured out round his feet. "I could pay with a story."

While Atticus finished his last mouthful of bread and cheese eight pairs of eyes watched him expectantly.

He cleared his throat. "A good meal deserves a good tale!" he said. "I'll tell you the story of a great flood."

 The children wriggled closer and settled down to listen.

The Greatest Flood

Prometheus had a son called Deucalion, who was good and kind. He loved all the birds and beasts and insects – he even loved the eagle who tore at his father's liver each morning.

"He's only doing his job!" he would say to poor Prometheus, on his yearly visit to the Caucasus.

And Prometheus would grit his teeth and nod bravely, as Deucalion stroked the eagle's feathers while they talked.

But one year, Prometheus was brought some terrible tidings by the North Wind. He begged the eagle to take a day off to fetch Deucalion to him.

And because Deucalion had been kind to him, the eagle went.

"My son," said Prometheus, "you must save yourself and your wife. Zeus is angry with Pandora for opening my jar and letting all the evils into the world. They have infected my clay people, and now they are being so cruel to each other that Zeus is going to get rid of them. He is going to make it rain and rain, till all the earth is covered, and everything in it is drowned. You must make a boat for yourself and Pyrrha and then you will escape."

"But Father, what about all the animals and birds and insects? They aren't like your people – they are innocent. How can I save them?" asked Deucalion.

So Prometheus told him how to build a great ark, with enough room for two of each kind of creature.

And soon the whole earth was covered in water, and the only things alive upon it were Deucalion and his wife, and the creatures they had gathered into the ark.

It was very smelly, and there wasn't much food, but after nine nights and days the waters went down, and the ark came to land on the top of a great mountain.

The animals and birds and insects scampered and flew and crawled off to find new homes, and Deucalion and Pyrrha knelt on the land and praised Zeus for their escape.

They lit a fire with some precious embers they had saved in a pot, and as the smoke reached up to Olympus, Zeus looked down and saw them praying.

"These are good people," he thought. "I shall help them."

So he gave a message to the North Wind, Boreas, and sent him to blow it into Deucalion's ear.

"Zeus says to throw the mother's bones over your shoulder!" whistled Boreas. Deucalion was very surprised. Surely Zeus didn't mean Pyrrha's bones.

"Zeus means the bones of Mother Earth, silly!" said Pyrrha.

And she picked up a big stone and threw it over her shoulder. Immediately, a little girl stood there. She came running up to Pyrrha to be hugged.

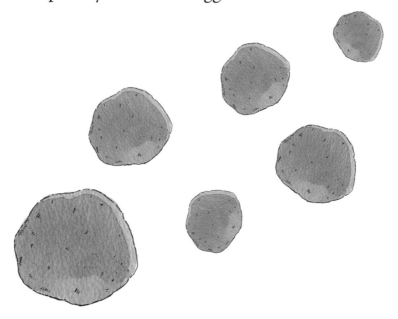

Deucalion and Pyrrha walked all over the earth throwing stones over their shoulders, and in each place they walked Deucalion made men and Pyrrha made women.

Some were brown and some were pink, and some were yellow and some were black.

And because they were made from stone, Pandora's evil stinging beasts were not nearly so harmful to them as they had been to the people Prometheus had made of clay so many years before.

Greek Beasts and Heroes and where to find them ...

In "The Stone Baby", Cronus married Rhea, the most beautiful of all the twelve Titans. Her brothers Atlas, Prometheus and Epimetheus also appeared in this book.

If you'd like to read about some of Rhea's sisters, why not look for clever Metis in "The Bee of Wisdom" which appears in *The Dolphin's Message*?

Or try "The Baby and the Cows" for the story of laughing Maia, the smallest Titan. (You can find her in *The Silver Chariot*.)

 76

When poor, wounded Uranus went running off into the outer darkness of heaven, three drops of his blood fell to earth, and  one into the sea. What happened next?

You'll have to read the stories of "The Kindly Ones" and "The Foam Goddess" to find out! So look out for them in *The Silver Chariot* and *The Magic Head*.

Atticus's stories are full of monstrous monsters! Are you brave enough to meet some more?

The Flying Horse tells tales of the hero Heracles who had to fight the many-headed Hydra in a smelly swamp, and of Bellerophon and Pegasus who flew off together to kill the fiery snake-tailed Chimaera.

Go on, you're not scared really, are you?

 77

Greek Beasts and Heroes
Collect them all!

From February 2010:

1. The Beasts in the Jar
2. The Magic Head
3. The Monster in the Maze
4. The Dolphin's Message

From May 2010:

5. The Silver Chariot
6. The Fire Breather
7. The Flying Horse
8. The Harp of Death

From August 2010:

9. The Dragon's Teeth
10. The Hero's Spear
11. The One-Eyed Giant
12. The Sailor Snatchers